# LEMBA JEWISH RIGHTS

## A case for Religious Freedom

KEN TECUMSEH SIBANDA, ESQ

For my late mother - Lucia, and my late father - Andrew.

Lalibela Press

# Introduction

The Supreme Court Justice William Rehnquist opined in his famous dictum that no matter how much law can equate the African American with the Caucasian, 'it's very unlikely that white Americans will ever accept African Americans regardless of the mount of law legislated.' He was mistaken on two accounts; the first is that he imagined white Americans to be too much like him and the second is that no man can really predict the resultant culture when law is passed. As far as I know history proved him wrong and Obama was elected as President in 2008.

My point is that the manner of racial prejudice tends, to be historically exaggerated, the gaps between black and white stems from misunderstandings that arise from ignorance, economic and historic facts; as well as systemic structural expectations – one race lies and another tells the truth for example. That said, a starting point is perhaps a neutrally accepted fact upon which interpretation can then be made.

The discourse between African Jews and White / European Jews (mainly Ashkenazi) is essentially about a fact – are you Jews? In the course of this book, I will show that indeed African Jews do exist and their right to practice religion stems from racial ignorance of this fact. They should neither be made to jump hoops to attain acceptance but instead need to be accepted and help in learning the Torah and practicing their religion, the African Jews conversion to any sect of the Ashkenazim must not be forced but voluntarily if the African Jew feels a need to belong to that particular sect.

I will address the matrilineal debate in who is a Jew later in chapter one. Bur briefly this stems from an ill conceived notion that a Jewish mother can only produce a Jewish child or knows of her Jewish child, whether in the Torah, Mishnah or other learned writings this first takes root will be further examined.

According to the Torah, the Jew is a descendant of the

Hebrew Israelite; by descent or Abrahamic faith; those who came out of Egypt, and is taken from the name Judah – he is an Israelite, this is accepted by every one. The other type of Jew is the Levi, and from that is the high Priest, the Kohanim.

Where the gates diverge is where Rabbis interpreted Jewishness as a matrilineal concept for the original Hebrew Israelite. Was this an acknowledgement of the link with the original Hebrew Israelite being lost and the establishment of parameters for the new practitioners of Judaism who wanted, for good reason, to protect the new Israelite congregation under God? And yet this was against the backdrop that the Kohanim or the high priest was ordained through the patrilineal line.

If indeed there was such a huge need for a matrilineal inheritance the Torah would have started as such since all the Law and laws are presently stated in it. Perhaps, the more pointed question is why there is a human need to add to the Torah and as such create tensions and divisions not stated in the Torah and more pointedly as given to Moshe Rabbeinu (Moses) ( peace be upon his name): the first Rabbi.

However there is a good point of having Jewish mothers point who is their child and who is not, and that preliminary enumeration should always be factored in any discourse on what is family. But once a woman's ancestor convert to Judaism, that requirement should be lifted for her subsequent generations especially when a patrilineal line is clearly traceable in her husband through DNA and she is married to a Jew. It is unfair and sexist to expect that the African female convert should convert until she arrives in Israel for her final Conversion.

To argue that every generation (female) of a converted woman's descendants, fifty generations ago or so to present, should have personally converted to Judaism to satisfy the matrilineal requirement is grossly unfair and creates a freedom of religion issue.

Our justice system has included brilliant minds; brilliant men and women who were sometimes given to overlooking facts of life, and instead emphasized the

poorly presented facts by the attorney's in front of
them. I will try as much, to present the case for African
Jews in the most objective manner and with the most
supporting facts so that the reader can see why
rabbinical laws in Israel should be reformed. By
reformed I mean a gradual understanding of the world as
it exists now, and not a dry world stored in the scribbles
of history books.

The right to practice one's religion is enshrined in the
United States Constitution first amendment as the right
to free exercise clause. When the founding fathers

decided on this amendemment in 1827, it was to include

the many varied voices in American society: the Quaker,

the Protestant, the Catholic and many other important

voices who were at that time engaged in a popular

discourse for political leverage. In this sense, what is

primed from the African experience is that modifications

are possible, if not permissible in an evolving world or

system.

This is the backdrop to a wider scale of discussion, around

the world many countries and nations are still to catch

up with this right. A right in the tradition of what is

termed in Latin in pari operatio – as operating on its own

or in common Law terms, a Human Right. Recently, in the past decade, there has been a rapid emergence of a group that deserves closer attention by any follower of international constitutional rights – the African Jew. For their emergence on the world scale marks a change in the body-politic of the Jewish family as well as the aspirant theology of that group. The air-lifting of the last Ethiopian Jews in the 80s' to Israel and the subsequent racism (employment; forced conversion; social expectations etc) they faced in Israel is also a relevant backdrop.

A recent news article had reported that twice Ethiopian Jewish women were given the birth control without heir permission in immigration holding camps; Ethiopian Jews are discriminated against in all walks of life in Israel – but mostly in housing, education and employment. While on face value operation Moses was a success when one interviews Ethiopian Jews one quickly realizes that they are increasingly been drawn into a civil rights corner, right in the heart of the Holy land.

This area of popular discourse has been greatly hurt by people who hurriedly seek to accomplish what looks like a life's career in just a mere summation of articles and books. In Nelson Mandela's words – the struggle is my life: it is vital for emerging discourse on African Jews to let and support African Jews speaking for themselves. Just as institutions have supported, Lithuanian Jews,

East European Jews, survivors of the Holocaust, so forth and so on. We cannot have a credible historic record until the subject is given access and a platform. For it was up to the South Africans headed by Nelson Mandela to find their voice, the Americans under George Washington and the British under Churchill. Each era dictates a person(s) to assist in the promulgation of interests subsisting within communal ties. For the Lemba, Professor Mathiviha has helped us in gaining the needed traction for our struggle as legitimate Jews. The struggle for African Jewry must be lead, informed and undertaken by African Jews. To quote the poet Amie Ceasare – there are no easy victories.

As a note to the reader, I am an African Jew – a lemba

from South Africa. And trace my ancestry through my father to the Buba Clan. Buba it would appear was a Kohanim who closely associated himself, for what ever reason, with the tribe of Judah since he offered leadership, as nominally Judah does; but his leadership was not political (since to this day the Lemba have no centralized leadership but ritualistic and divine leadership) a unique reality; a high priest in the tribe of Judah – this is how the narrative of the Lemba Hebrews started. My mother came from the Shona speaking Lemba who have their nucleus in Mberengwa in Zimbabwe and was born in Kwekwe, with her maiden name being Taruvinga. My father was born in South Africa, East London and had been closely associated with the Lemba in the Limpopo Province. Sibanda, my last name is an alliteration which means "lion" in various Zimbabwean tribal dialects (Kalanga, Ndebele, Zulu, Xhosa). I was raised in a home that spoke fluent Xhosa and Shona.

For the Lemba we speak various languages but maintain the Judaic practices as passed down by our ancestor Abraham. We believe in One God (Nwali), in the Messianic age and in ties to other world Jews as brothers and sisters. We maintain kosher diet and try as much to marry within the tribe. Even when two people speak different languages it is possible from discernment that these two are Lemba since we speak, of late, most of the South African languages, as well as Shona – spoken in Zimbabwe.

I use the term African Jew and not black Jew because the term black is misnomer in this case. When speaking of racial genes only three species exist in the human family; the Caucasian, the Mongoloid and the African. So far the Jew has come from the Caucasian family of genes; this is what is known as the Ashkenazi Jew. But recent DNA evidence, sequenced in England and carried out by various scientist hints that the Jewish Y Chromosome is traceable in to another Sephardic group, the African, in particularly the Lemba; thus making him a genetic Jew albeit within the African family.

This does not rule out the other African Jews who were not tested – The Beta Israel and the Igbo's. It is only a matter of time until their oral history is vindicated, their cause will be discussed later in this book.

However, the social milieu of history and practice dictates that this precarious position of the African Jew is digested in the context of present day Jewry. What indeed, are the rights of African Jews in a world that is already defined? In a world where they start off, as outsiders and journey inward, if not outwardly towards Jerusalem. I argue that the African right is one of complete unadulterated simplicity – the right to religious freedom. It is a right that is deeply rooted in what Cato termed the ethos of state or the functions of state institutions. A right that is upheld in any modern civilized Nation.

What African Jews are not considered Jews: is the synthesis of newer forms of racism, the mirrored face of racism and the ugly caricatures of anti-Semitic discourse. We are not black-faced Jews, nor are we appendages to preexisting narrative; we demand to be defined by our own history and persons. We are certainly not the Guinea pig of untested new Rabbinic insights and laws; the thesis paper (or book) of a marauding college professor; we are not cartoons, nor are we the platform for debate – ours is a human right, that flows into constitutional rights thus becoming a Civil Right to be maintained and policed by law. African Jews are a people, like any other with a right to their religion.

First things first, who exactly are the African Jews?

The right to practice one's religion is central to socio-

economic wellbeing of any group. At the root or ground

norm is the essential understanding that – this is how

this people see themselves and in the alternate should

be seen by other groups. It makes the difference

between the choice of black and African, between

Sardinian and Italian between Xhosa or Red people. It

consolidates a people's folklore and oral record of its

genesis.

Writing on Vietnam, the late attorney general Robert Kennedy, made the observation that dealing with the Viet Cong was difficult, and no American could penetrate the bond that existed between the average Vietcong and Ngo Hein 'since Ngo Hein – is a Viet Cong,' said senator Kennedy.

This realization should not be limited to thru late Senator, but applies in regard to our modern understanding of the bonds between folklore and its people. It is difficult to separate and come between a people and their oral record, and attempt leads to endless strive and tension.

Religious tension is not limited to African Jews and Caucasian / European Jews – such tension also exists for the Christian. Most churches (with the exception of some Catholic churches and Evangelical organizations) remain segregated. It is an open secret that there are white Churches and Black churches.

Thus where law has succeeded in the economic sphere to bridge gaps between blacks and whites, ironically in Religion the gap is growing with these 'whites only' and 'black only' places of workshop – where in the Bible does it advocate for separate and divided worship?

The neighbor, in any event, may take on any color or race. Religion is an area that must be integrated sooner or later, especially given the very key tenet of love your neighbor that it preaches. The definitive step or building block to a person's participation in civic society is

identity and religion plays a huge part, - not education,

marriage not cultural habits.

CHAPTERS


1. Legal Theory


2. A History of African Jews

3. A History of the Problem




4. The Right to Religious Freedom




5. The Present Context of Rabbinical Assimilation




6. The Road ahead for African Jews

Booklet series

PAGE xxi

[ For full book contact publisher at publsiher@proteusfilm.com.

www.ingramcontent.com/pod-product-compliance
Lightning Source LLC
Chambersburg PA
CBHW021000180526
45163CB00006B/2444